blueberry

guava

pear

apple

pear

strawberry

banana

plum

orange

look and cook

BREAKFAST

a first
book of
recipes
in
pictures

valorie fisher

ASTRA YOUNG READERS

AN IMPRINT OF ASTRA BOOKS FOR YOUNG READERS

New York

Look and Cook was created with young chefs in mind, those who might not yet be confident readers but are adventurous eaters and enthusiastic helpers in the kitchen. Through simple pictures, these visual recipes allow kids to understand and follow each step that goes into preparing a given food. This unique cookbook format encourages independence and means kids can take the lead in the kitchen, asking for assistance as they need it. Of course, we do recommend adults support kid chefs as they follow these recipes, especially in gathering ingredients and equipment beforehand and giving help whenever they see .

Kids will enjoy the process, the math, the mess, the magic, the cleanup (maybe), and, of course, sharing what they've created!

 **2**   Servings or amount the recipe makes

 10 minutes   Time needed for the recipe or a step

    Step supervised or done by a grown-up

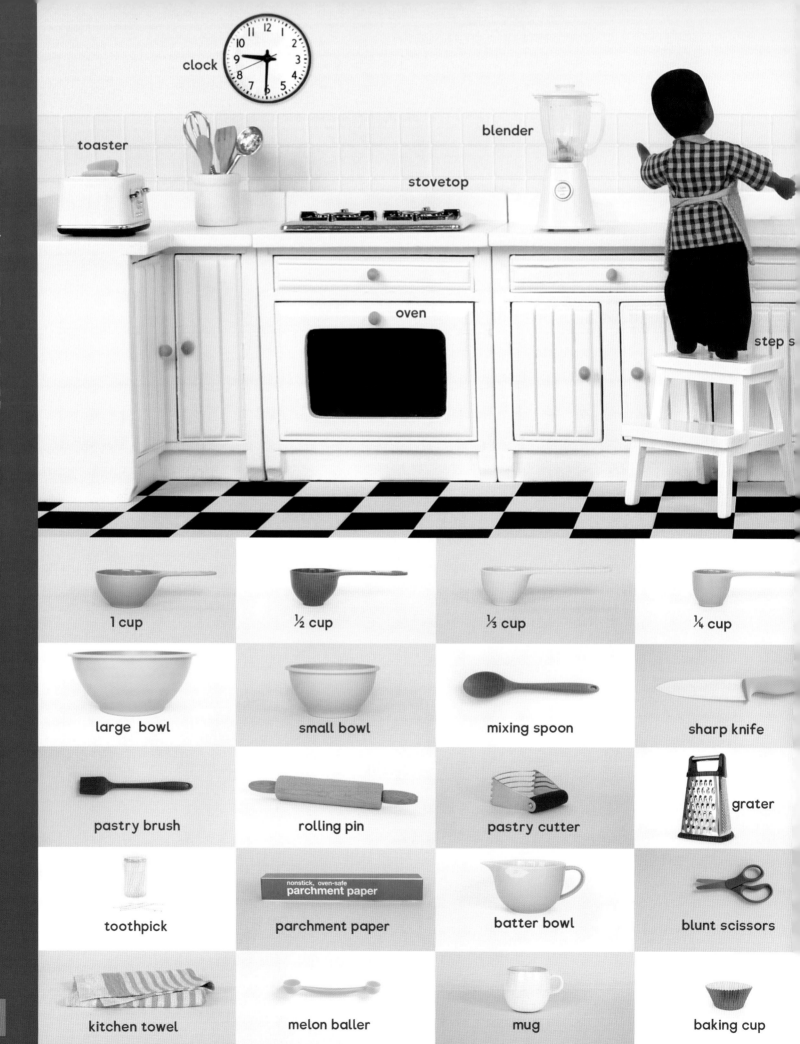

clock

toaster

blender

stovetop

oven

step s

1 cup

½ cup

⅓ cup

¼ cup

large bowl

small bowl

mixing spoon

sharp knife

pastry brush

rolling pin

pastry cutter

grater

toothpick

nonstick, oven-safe
parchment paper

parchment paper

batter bowl

blunt scissors

kitchen towel

melon baller

mug

baking cup

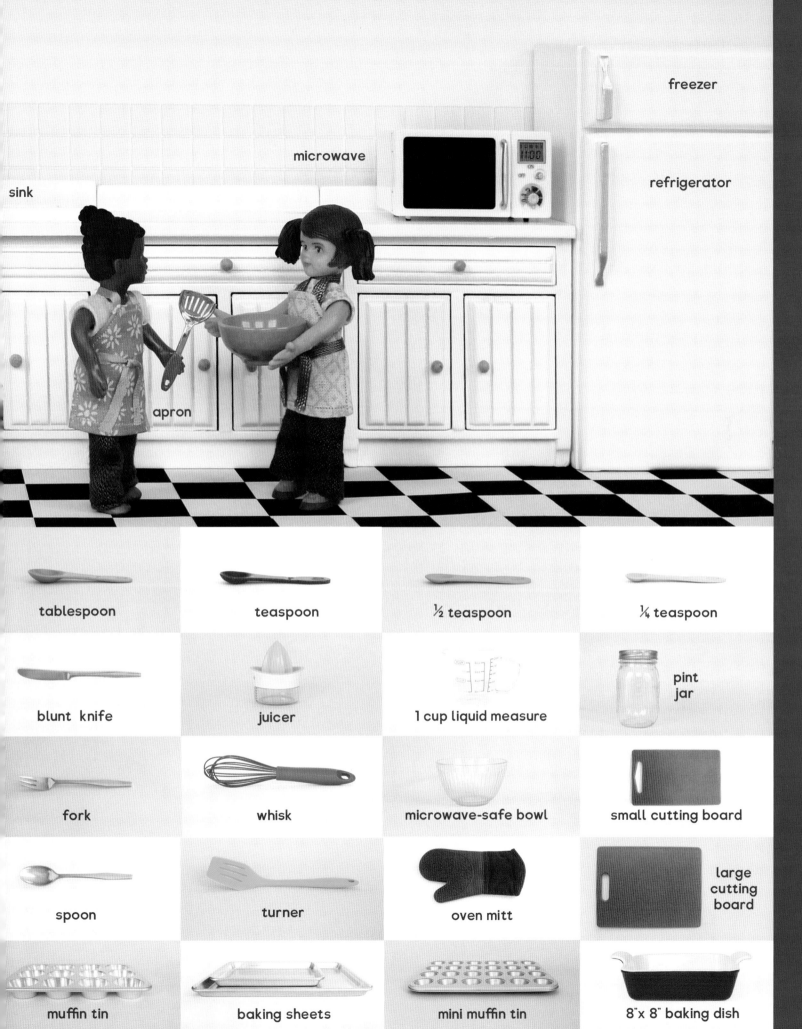

sink

microwave

freezer

refrigerator

apron

tablespoon

teaspoon

½ teaspoon

¼ teaspoon

blunt knife

juicer

1 cup liquid measure

pint jar

fork

whisk

microwave-safe bowl

small cutting board

spoon

turner

oven mitt

large cutting board

muffin tin

baking sheets

mini muffin tin

8"x 8" baking dish

Read the recipe

Wash your hands

Wash all fruits and vegetables

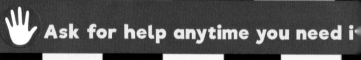 Ask for help anytime you need i

Gather your kitchen tools

Gather your ingredients

Have fun

Help clean up

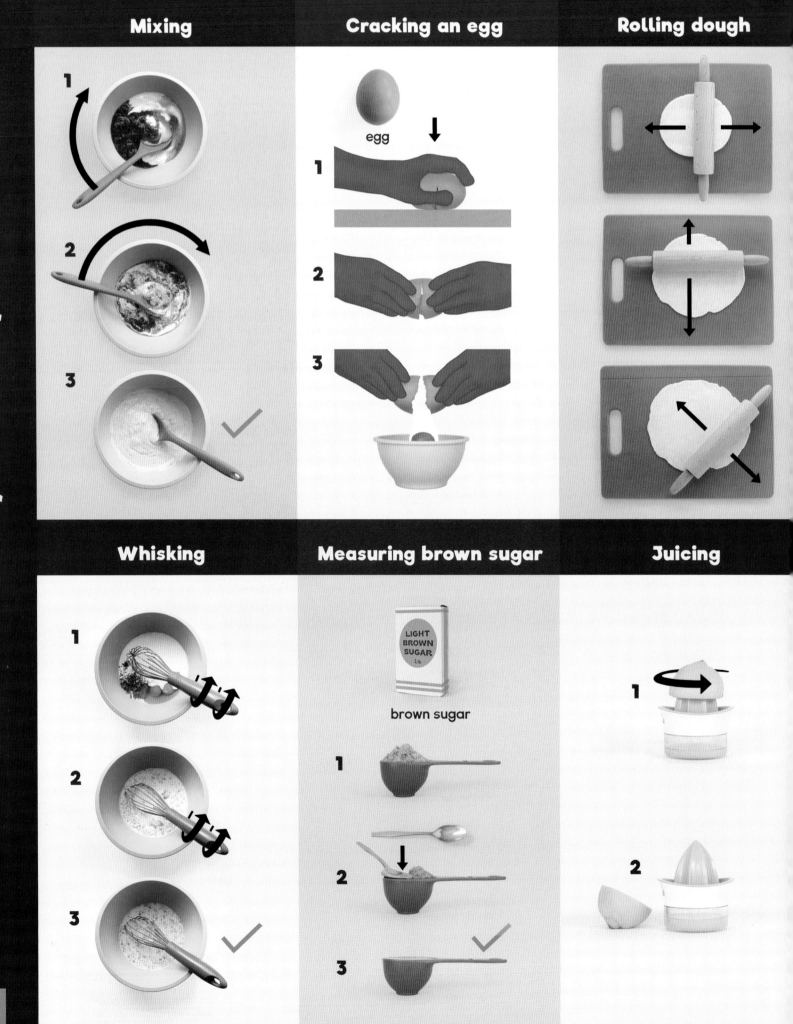

Mixing

1
2
3

Cracking an egg

egg

1
2
3

Rolling dough

Whisking

1
2
3

Measuring brown sugar

LIGHT BROWN SUGAR
1 lb

brown sugar

1
2
3

Juicing

1
2

Measuring butter

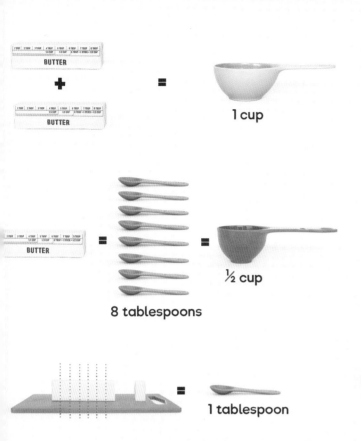

BUTTER + BUTTER = 1 cup

BUTTER = 8 tablespoons = ½ cup

= 1 tablespoon

Measuring cups and spoons

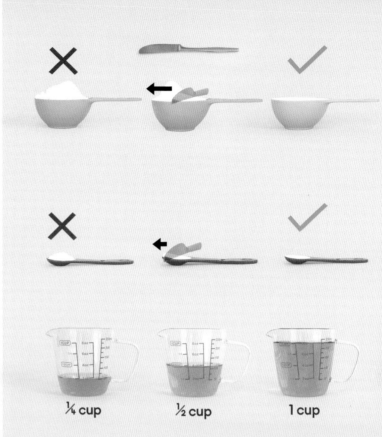

✗ ✓

✗ ✓

¼ cup   ½ cup   1 cup

Pinch of salt

Snipping herbs

Baking toothpick test

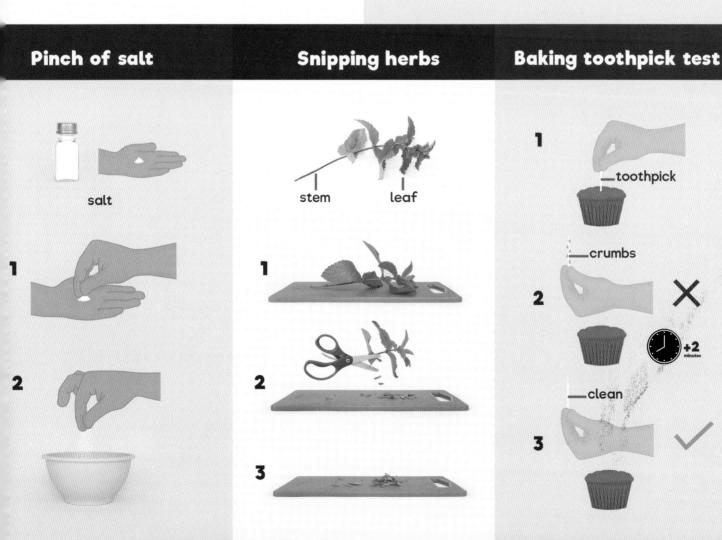

salt

1

2

stem   leaf

1

2

3

1

—toothpick

—crumbs

2 ✗

+2 minutes

—clean

3 ✓

LEMON BEE TEA

5 minutes

water

2 tablespoons lemon juice

1 lemon slice

2 tablespoons honey

small cutting board

1 tablespoon

spoon

juicer

sharp knife

mug

microwave

1

2

3

4

5

6

COCOA CUP

  1

 **5 minutes**

milk

2 teaspoons cocoa

1 tablespoon honey

1 teaspoon

1 tablespoon

spoon

mug

microwave

1

+

2

3

4

5

6

SMOOTH BLUE

 1

1 banana

1 cup
frozen blueberries

1 cup

blender

1

2

3

BERRY BAGEL

½ bagel

cream cheese

3 strawberries

sharp knife

blunt knife

small cutting board

1

2

3

4

BEAR POOP

 1    **10** minutes

⅓ cup
frozen mixed berries

1 tablespoon
maple syrup

¼ cup granola ✳

½ cup
plain Greek yogurt

✳ make your own granola **CRANOLA** 16

¼ cup

1 tablespoon

½ cup

⅓ cup

microwave-safe bowl

microwave

✳ **BEAR POOP** is also delicious with
SLEEPOVER OATS 18
and **PANCAKE BUTTONS!** 32

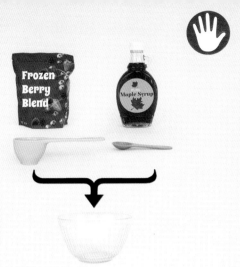

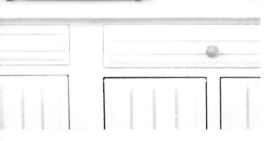

2

5 minutes

3

plain YOGURT 6oz

4

CRUNCHY GRANOLA 12 OZ

5

6

TASTY TOAST

1

15 minutes

½ ripe avocado

slice of bread

½ teaspoon lemon juice

½ teaspoon everything bagel seasoning

1 teaspoon pepitas

sharp knife

fork

spoon

½ teaspoon

1 teaspoon

small cutting board

juicer

small bowl

toaster

 ✗  ✗  ✗  ✓ ✗

14

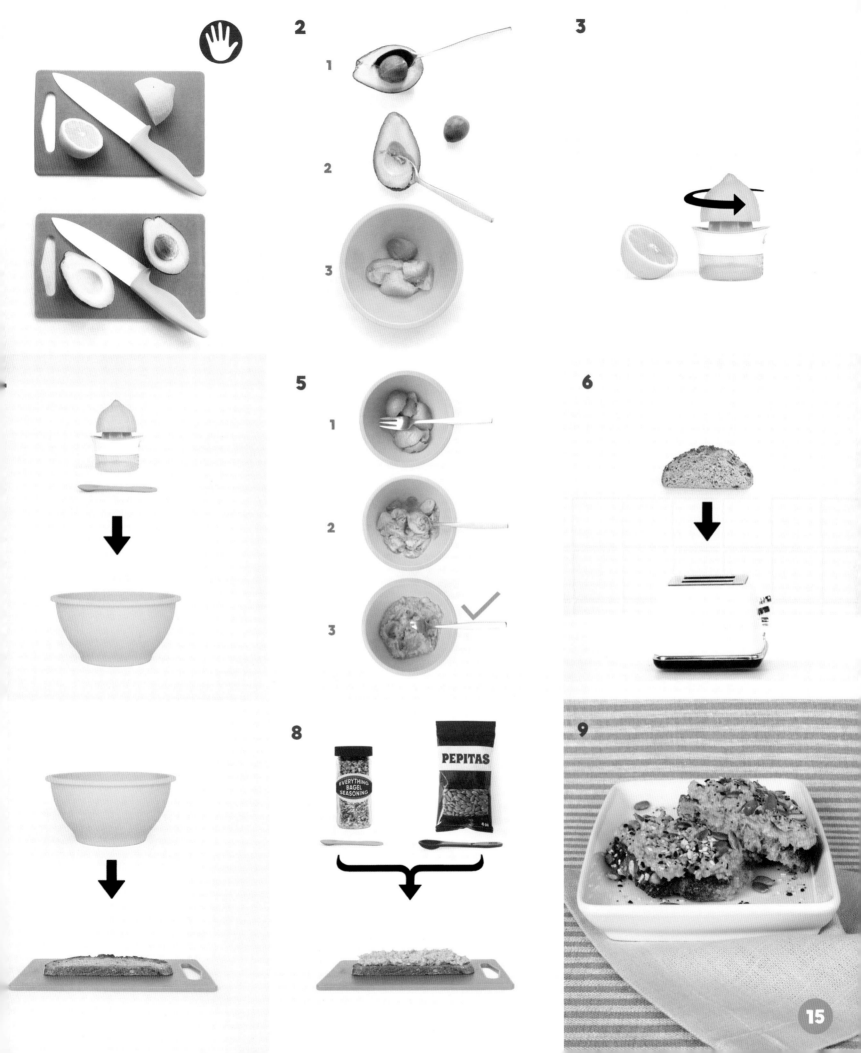

CRANOLA

3 cups rolled oats

1 cup sliced almonds

1 cup unsweetened coconut flake

⅓ cup coconut oil

½ cup honey

1 tablespoon cinnamon

½ cup pepitas

1 cup dried cranberries

1 cup

½ cup

⅓ cup

1 tablespoon

turner

microwave-safe bowl

mixing spoon

oven mitt

parchment paper

baking sheet

large bowl

microwave

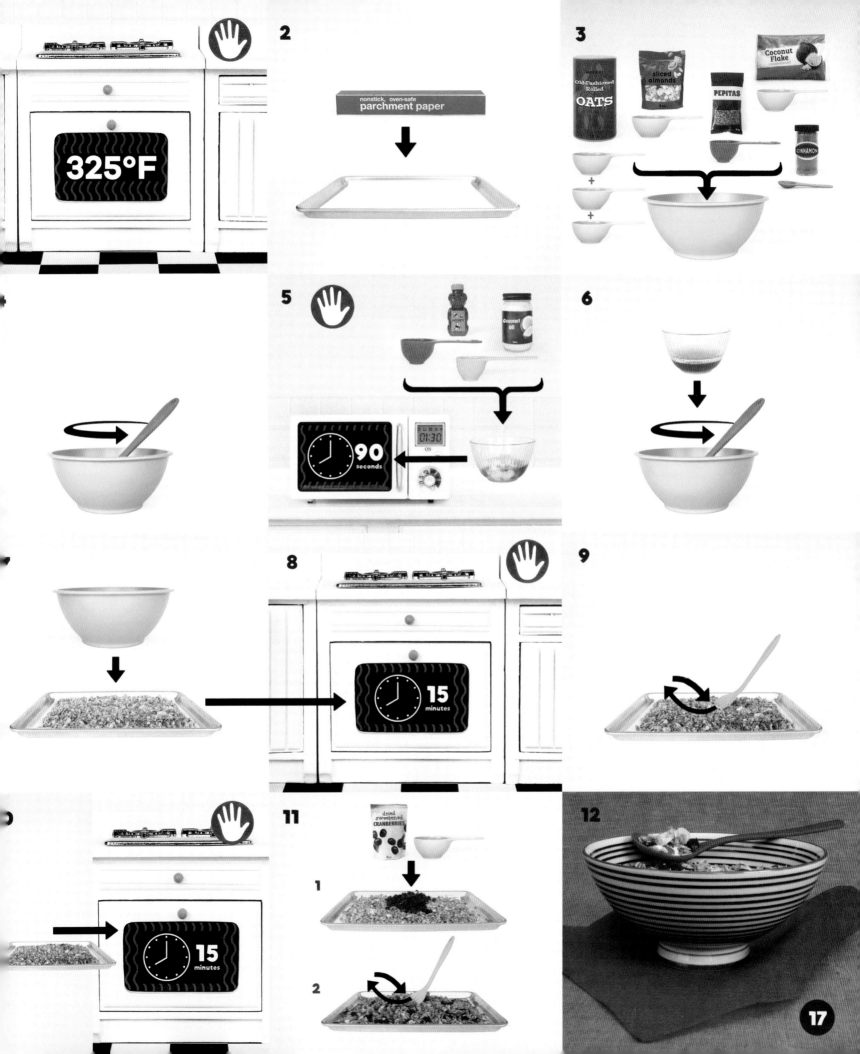

2 nonstick, oven-safe parchment paper

3 OATS · sliced almonds · PEPITAS · Coconut Flake · CINNAMON

5 HONEY · Coconut Oil · 90 seconds · 01:30 ON

6

8 15 minutes

9

11
dried sweetened CRANBERRIES
1
2

12

17

SLEEPOVER OATS

 1

 **10** minutes **+** overnight

| ½ cup rolled oats | ¾ cup milk | 1 tablespoon honey | 1 tablespoon chia seeds |

½ cup   1 tablespoon

1 cup liquid measure   spoon   pint jar

1

2

3

1   2

4

overnight

Add different toppings to your SLEEPOVER OATS!

3 strawberries

1 tablespoon
sliced almonds

¼ cup blueberries

1 tablespoon
unsweetened coconut flake

1 tablespoon granola
✳ make your own granola **CRANOLA** 16

1 tablespoon raisins

½ banana

1 tablespoon
chopped walnuts

CINNAMON SPRINKLE

 1  **10** minutes

2 tablespoons cinnamon	½ cup sugar	soft butter	slice of bread

1 tablespoon	blunt knife	spoon

½ cup	small bowl	toaster

* save leftover **CINNAMON SPRINKLE** for tomorrow's toast

1

2

3

4

5

BERRY BANANA BLAST

 1

 **10** minutes

¾ cup frozen mixed berries

1 banana

¼ cup plain yogurt

1 tablespoon almond butter

¼ cup granola ✳

blender

¼ cup

1 tablespoon

✳ make your own granola **CRANOLA** 16

1

2

3

4

5

6

FRUIT RIOT

2 cups
honeydew balls

2 clementines

1 banana

2 tablespoon
lemon juice

1 cup
raspberries

1 cup
blueberries

1 tablespoon
honey

6
mint leave

1 tablespoon

melon baller

1 cup

blunt knife

juicer

sharp knife

blunt scissors

mixing spoon

large cutting board

large bowl

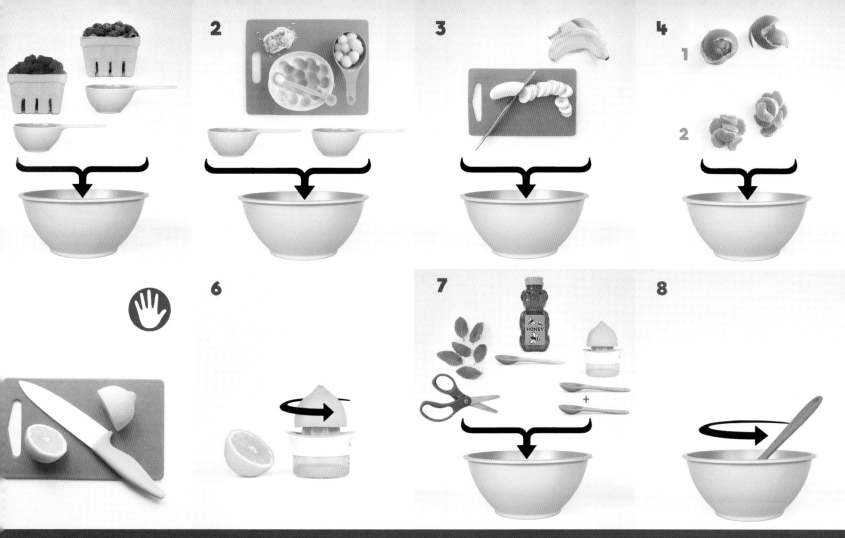

Mix it up with different fruits!

strawberry	apple	peach	mango	grapefruit
apricot	seedless grapes	watermelon	blackberry	cantaloupe
pear	pomegranate	orange	cherry	kiwi

23

TOPSY·TURVY EGGS

2 tablespoons milk

2 eggs

pinch of salt

1 tablespoon

fork

whisk

microwave-safe bowl

microwave

TEARABLE FRENCH TOAST

 4

 **55** minutes

1 cup
milk

7 thick
slices of bread

4 eggs

LIGHT BROWN SUGAR
3 tablespoons
light brown sugar

BUTTER
3 tablespoons
butter

CINNAMON
1 teaspoon
cinnamon

Pure Vanilla Extract
1 teaspoon
vanilla

1 teaspoon

whisk

pastry brush

microwave-safe
bowl

1 tablespoon

1 cup liquid measure

spoon

batter bowl

8" x 8" baking dish

microwave

oven mitt

26

27

CINNAMON SNAIL

12 **35 minutes**

1 tube biscuits

2 tablespoons butter

1 tablespoon cinnamon

⅓ cup light brown sugar

⅓ cup chopped pecans

1 tablespoon

blunt knife

rolling pin

⅓ cup

spoon

large cutting board

pastry brush

small bowl

muffin tin

microwave-safe bowl

microwave

oven mitt

BLUFFIN

 12

 45 minutes

1½ cup
blueberries

1½ cup
flour

½ cup
sugar

1 egg

5 tablespoons
butter

2 teaspoons
baking powder

¾ cup
plain yogurt

¼ teaspoon
salt

¼ cup
turbinado sugar

¼ teaspoon

1 teaspoon

spoon

mixing spoon

¼ cup

½ cup

1 cup

12 baking cups

microwave-safe bowl

large bowl

toothpick

microwave

muffin tin

oven mitt

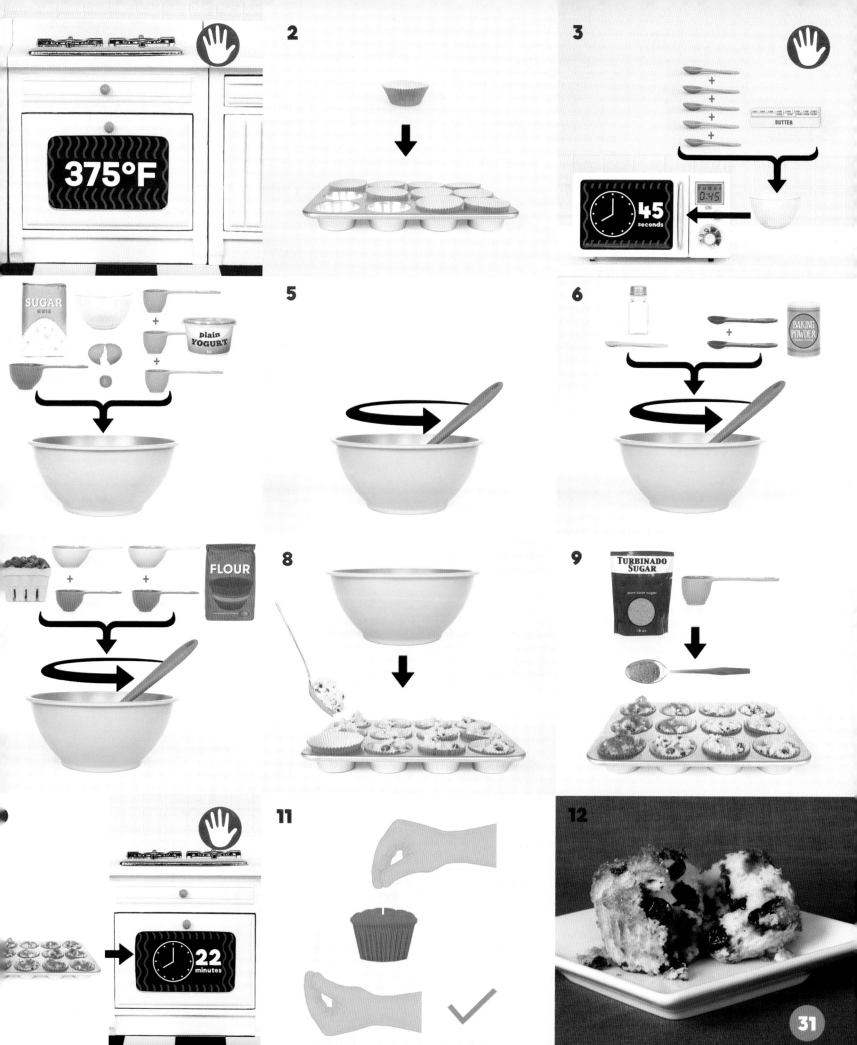

375°F

2

3

45 seconds

SUGAR

plain YOGURT

5

6

BAKING POWDER

FLOUR

8

9

TURBINADO SUGAR
pure cane sugar
16 oz

22 minutes

11

PANCAKE BUTTONS

 24

 20 minutes

½ cup
flour

½ cup
buttermilk

1 tablespoon
sugar

1 tablespoon
canola oil

3 tablespoons
butter

1 egg

1 teaspoon
baking powder

1 tablespoon

1 teaspoon

spoon

whisk

pastry brush

mini muffin tin

½ cup

1 cup liquid measure

microwave-safe bowl

large bowl

microwave

oven mitt

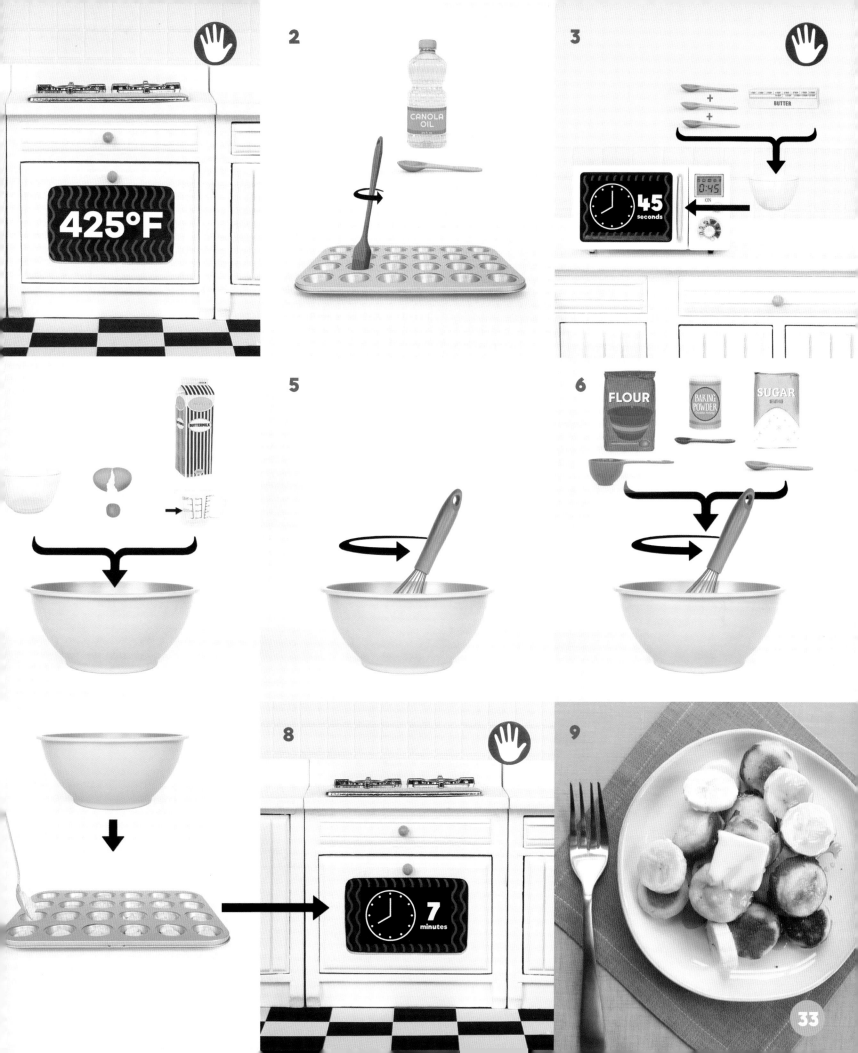

1 425°F

2

3 0:45 / 45 seconds

5

6

8 7 minutes

9

33

CHOCO PILLOW

 8

 1 hour

1 sheet frozen puff pastry

3-ounce bar dark chocolate

1 egg

1 tablespoon water

1 tablespoon

blunt knife

pastry brush

whisk

small bowl

large cutting board

parchment paper

parchment paper

baking sheet

oven mitt

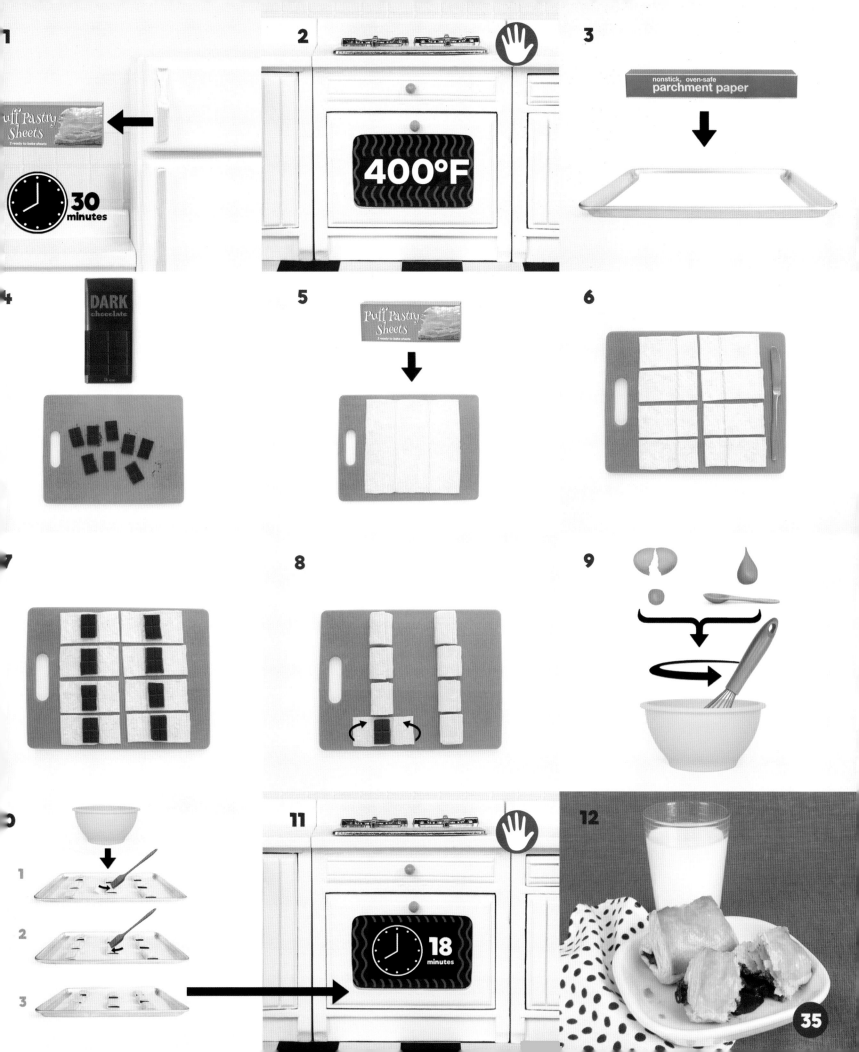

1 Puff Pastry Sheets — 30 minutes

2 400°F

3 nonstick, oven-safe parchment paper

4 DARK chocolate

5 Puff Pastry Sheets

6

7

8

9

10
1
2
3

11 18 minutes

12

EGG BOMB

6

40 minutes

5 eggs

6 tablespoons shredded cheddar cheese

6 ham slices

1 tablespoon olive oil

¼ teaspoon salt

2 tablespoons chives

¼ teaspoon

1 tablespoon

blunt scissors

whisk

batter bowl

pastry brush

muffin tin

oven mitt

350°F

2

3

5

SLICED
VIRGINIA HAM

6

CHEDDAR
shredded cheese

8

23
minutes

9

WAKIE FLAKIES

 9

 **30 minutes**

2 cups flour

5 tablespoons butter

2 tablespoons baking powder

1 teaspoon salt

1 cup milk

1 cup

1 teaspoon

1 tablespoon

blunt knife

1 cup liquid measure

pastry cutter

mixing spoon

oven mitt

large cutting board

parchment paper

rolling pin

large bowl

baking sheet

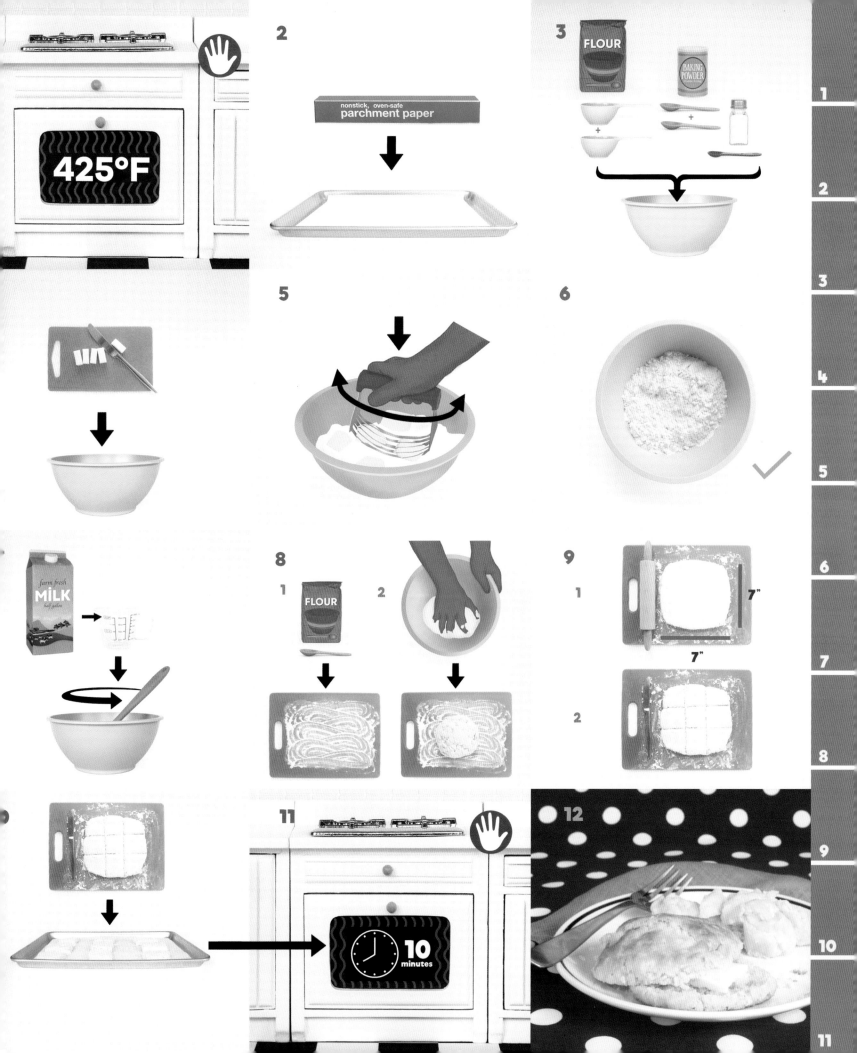

ZUCUFFIN

 12

 45 minutes

1 cup grated zucchini

¾ cup flour

⅓ cup light brown sugar

¼ cup canola oil

¼ teaspoon cinnamon

1 egg

¼ teaspoon baking powder

¼ teaspoon baking soda

¼ cup dried cranberries

¼ teaspoon salt

½ cup chopped walnuts

grater

toothpick

¼ teaspoon

¼ cup

blunt knife

spoon

⅓ cup

12 baking cups

½ cup

mixing spoon

1 cup

oven mitt

1 cup liquid measure

muffin tin

small cutting board

large bowl

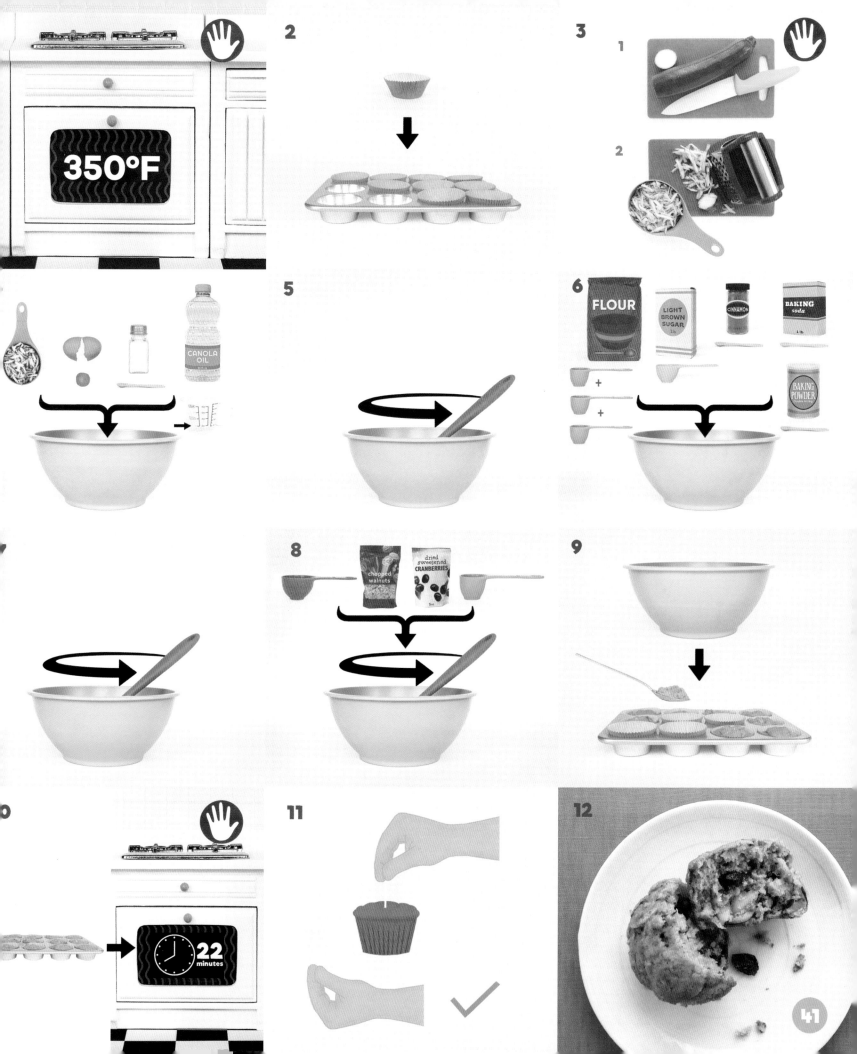

350°F

2

3
1
2

5

6

FLOUR LIGHT BROWN SUGAR CINNAMON BAKING soda

+
+
BAKING POWDER

8
chopped walnuts dried sweetened CRANBERRIES

9

11

22 minutes

✓

MIX IT UP!

Missing an ingredient? Substitute!

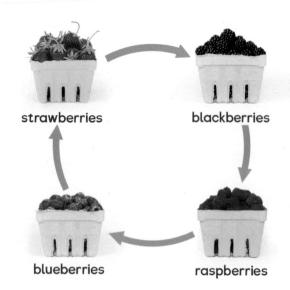

strawberries → blackberries → raspberries → blueberries → strawberries

frozen blueberries → frozen berry blend → frozen cherries → frozen blueberries

dark chocolate ↔ milk chocolate

pepitas ↔ sunflower seeds

Mix it up! Switch out ingredients!

EGG BOMB

shredded cheddar cheese

−

ham slices

+

6 tablespoons crumbled feta

honey

maple syrup

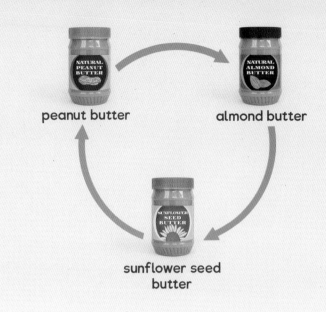

peanut butter

almond butter

sunflower seed
butter

dried cranberries

raisins

dried cherries

sliced almonds

chopped walnuts

chopped pecans

+   1 cup
baby spinach

OR

+   6 tablespoons
shredded mozzarella

+   ½ cup
cherry tomatoes halved

Breakfast with the family is simply the best.
For David, Aidan and Olive —VF

Astra Young Readers
An imprint of Astra Books for Young Readers,
a division of Astra Publishing House
astrapublishinghouse.com
Printed in China

ISBN: 978-1-6626-2068-3 (hc)
ISBN: 978-1-6626-2069-0 (eBook)
Library of Congress Control Number: 2023920527

First edition

10 9 8 7 6 5 4 3 2 1

Design by Valorie Fisher and Barbara Grzeslo
The text is set in Riffic Medium.
The titles are set in Riffic Bold.

Acknowledgments:
I am enormously grateful to Karen Hatt
for her insight and keen eye. I would like
to thank Susan Saccardi for sharing her
culinary wisdom; Jacque Schiller, Gina
Maolucci, Barbara Ensor, Georgia
Bambrick and Jacquie Strasburger for
their endless enthusiasm; Olive Cowan for
her word jumbling skills; and David Cowan
for his unflappable support. Last but not
least, a huge thanks to my terrific team
of recipe testers for the series, Hazel,
Theodora, Nat, Cam, Oliver and Ellis.

About the art in this book:
A photographer, set designer, and
adventurous home cook, Valorie Fisher
combined all of these skillsets to create
the photo illustrations in this book. Valorie
constructs miniature sets incorporating
kitchen tools, dollhouse miniatures, fruits,
vegetables, and other ingredients, and
then takes a picture.

apple

grapes

clementine

mango

pear

fig

orange

raspberry

blackberry